RAVENNA ITALY TRAVEL

GUIDE 2023

Everything you need to know

About how to discover

Ravenna and plan your trip.

Steven Reece.

GENERAL INTRODUCTION   7

CHAPTER 1: INTRODUCTION TO RAVENNA   9

- HISTORY: EXPLORE THE RICH HISTORICAL BACKGROUND OF RAVENNA, KNOWN FOR ITS SIGNIFICANT ROLE IN THE BYZANTINE EMPIRE.   9
- LOCATION AND ACCESSIBILITY: LEARN ABOUT RAVENNA'S GEOGRAPHICAL LOCATION AND THE VARIOUS WAYS TO REACH THIS ENCHANTING CITY.   9
- CLIMATE AND BEST TIME TO VISIT: DISCOVER THE IDEAL SEASONS TO EXPERIENCE RAVENNA'S PLEASANT WEATHER AND AVOID CROWDS   9

CHAPTER 2: TOP ATTRACTIONS IN RAVENNA   15

- BASILICA DI SAN VITALE: DELVE INTO THE ARCHITECTURAL MASTERPIECE ADORNED WITH STUNNING MOSAICS THAT DEPICT BIBLICAL SCENES.   15
- MAUSOLEUM OF GALLA PLACIDIA: EXPERIENCE THE EXQUISITE BEAUTY OF THIS MAUSOLEUM, RENOWNED FOR ITS SHIMMERING MOSAICS.   15
- DANTE'S TOMB: PAY HOMAGE TO THE FINAL RESTING PLACE OF THE FAMOUS POET DANTE ALIGHIERI, WHO FOUND REFUGE IN RAVENNA.   15
- BASILICA DI SANT'APOLLINARE IN CLASSE: EXPLORE THIS UNESCO WORLD HERITAGE SITE AND MARVEL AT ITS INTRICATE MOSAICS AND ANCIENT HISTORY. 15
- NEONIANO BAPTISTERY: DISCOVER THE OLDEST MONUMENT IN RAVENNA, FEATURING INTRICATE BAPTISMAL SCENES PORTRAYED THROUGH MOSAICS.   15

CHAPTER 3: CULTURAL AND HISTORICAL SITES 19

- MUSEO NAZIONALE DI RAVENNA: IMMERSE YOURSELF IN RAVENNA'S CULTURAL HERITAGE THROUGH A VISIT TO THIS MUSEUM, WHICH HOUSES AN IMPRESSIVE COLLECTION OF ARTIFACTS. 19
- ARIAN BAPTISTRY: UNCOVER THE REMNANTS OF THE ARIAN CHRISTIAN MOVEMENT AND ITS INFLUENCE ON RAVENNA'S HISTORY. 19
- ARCHIEPISCOPAL MUSEUM AND CHAPEL: DELIGHT IN THE ARTISTIC TREASURES PRESERVED WITHIN THIS MUSEUM, INCLUDING ILLUMINATED MANUSCRIPTS AND RELIGIOUS RELICS. 19
- ROCCA BRANCALEONE: LEARN ABOUT THE MILITARY HISTORY OF RAVENNA WHILE EXPLORING THIS MEDIEVAL FORTRESS. 19

CHAPTER 4: EXPLORING RAVENNA'S NEIGHBORHOODS 25

- RAVENNA CITY CENTER: STROLL THROUGH THE LIVELY STREETS AND PICTURESQUE SQUARES OF THE CITY CENTER, EXPERIENCING THE LOCAL ATMOSPHERE AND VIBRANT MARKETS. 25
- CLASSIS RAVENNA: DISCOVER THE ANCIENT ROMAN PORT OF RAVENNA, WITH ITS ARCHAEOLOGICAL REMAINS AND CAPTIVATING HISTORICAL SITES. 25
- MARINA DI RAVENNA: ESCAPE TO THE COAST AND ENJOY THE BEAUTIFUL BEACHES, WATERFRONT PROMENADES, AND FRESH SEAFOOD CUISINE. 25
- SANT'APOLLINARE: VISIT THE CHARMING VILLAGE SURROUNDING THE BASILICA, AND ADMIRE THE RURAL LANDSCAPES OF THE RAVENNA COUNTRYSIDE. 25

CHAPTER 5: GASTRONOMIC DELIGHTS OF RAVENNA   33

- LOCAL CUISINE: INDULGE IN RAVENNA'S TRADITIONAL DISHES, INCLUDING HOMEMADE PASTA, PIADINA (FLATBREAD), AND DELICIOUS SEAFOOD RECIPES.   33
- WINES AND WINERIES: EMBARK ON A JOURNEY THROUGH THE LOCAL VINEYARDS AND TASTE THE UNIQUE WINES PRODUCED IN THE REGION.   33
- PASTICCERIE: SAMPLE RAVENNA'S RENOWNED PASTRIES, SUCH AS THE AROMATIC CIAMBELLA AND THE SWEET DELICACY CALLED PIADA DOLCE.   33

CHAPTER 6: FESTIVALS AND EVENTS IN RAVENNA   41

- RAVENNA FESTIVAL: THE RAVENNA FESTIVAL IS A RENOWNED INTERNATIONAL EVENT THAT CELEBRATES THE ARTS IN ALL ITS FORMS.   41
- MOSAICO DI NOTTE: MOSAICO DI NOTTE, OR MOSAIC BY NIGHT, IS A UNIQUE EVENT THAT TAKES PLACE IN RAVENNA DURING THE SUMMER MONTHS   41
- FESTA DI SAN VITALE: THE FESTA DI SAN VITALE, CELEBRATED ON APRIL 28TH, IS A RELIGIOUS FESTIVAL DEDICATED TO RAVENNA'S PATRON SAINT, SAINT VITALIS.   41
- ROMBI DI PASSIONE: ROMBI DI PASSIONE, OR RHOMBUSES OF PASSION, IS A MEDIEVAL FESTIVAL THAT TAKES PLACE IN THE VILLAGE OF SANT'APOLLINARE, JUST OUTSIDE RAVENNA.   41
- RAVENNA NIGHTMARE FILM FESTIVAL: FOR HORROR MOVIE ENTHUSIASTS, THE RAVENNA NIGHTMARE FILM FESTIVAL IS A MUST-ATTEND EVENT.   41

CHAPTER 7: PRACTICAL INFORMATION AND TRAVEL TIPS 47

- BOLOGNA: VENTURE BEYOND RAVENNA AND EXPLORE THE VIBRANT CITY OF BOLOGNA, FAMOUS FOR ITS RICH HISTORY, CUISINE, AND MEDIEVAL ARCHITECTURE. 47
- FERRARA: VISIT THIS CHARMING RENAISSANCE CITY, KNOWN FOR ITS WELL-PRESERVED HISTORIC CENTER AND IMPOSING ESTE CASTLE. 47
- SAN MARINO: TAKE A TRIP TO THE INDEPENDENT MICROSTATE OF SAN MARINO 47

CHAPTER 8: DAY TRIPS FROM RAVENNA 55

- BOLOGNA: LOCATED JUST A SHORT TRAIN RIDE AWAY FROM RAVENNA, BOLOGNA IS A VIBRANT CITY KNOWN FOR ITS HISTORIC ARCHITECTURE, CULINARY DELIGHTS, AND LIVELY ATMOSPHERE. 55
- FERRARA: ANOTHER CHARMING CITY WITHIN REACH OF RAVENNA IS FERRARA. FAMOUS FOR ITS WELL-PRESERVED RENAISSANCE ARCHITECTURE AND IMPRESSIVE ESTE CASTLE, FERRARA OFFERS A GLIMPSE INTO ITALY'S GLORIOUS PAST 55
- RIMINI: FOR THOSE SEEKING A BEACHSIDE ESCAPE, RIMINI IS AN EXCELLENT CHOICE. KNOWN FOR ITS LONG SANDY BEACHES AND VIBRANT NIGHTLIFE 55
- SAN MARINO: A SHORT JOURNEY FROM RAVENNA WILL TAKE YOU TO THE TINY AND INDEPENDENT REPUBLIC OF SAN MARINO, ONE OF THE WORLD'S OLDEST SURVIVING SOVEREIGN STATES 55

- BRISIGHELLA: LOCATED IN THE APENNINE MOUNTAINS, BRISIGHELLA IS A CHARMING MEDIEVAL VILLAGE WITH A DISTINCTIVE THREE-PEAKED HILL.   55

CHAPTER 9: TIPS FOR A MEMORABLE STAY IN RAVENNA   60

- PLAN AHEAD   60
- GUIDED TOURS   60
- EXPLORE ON FOOT OR BY BIKE   60
- SAMPLE LOCAL CUISINE   60
- VISIT LESSER-KNOWN ATTRACTIONS   60
- USE PUBLIC TRANSPORTATION OR WALK...   60

CHAPTER 10. CONCLUSION AND RECOMMENDATION   65

- CONCLUSION: RAVENNA IS A CITY THAT CAPTIVATES VISITORS WITH ITS RICH HISTORY, BREATHTAKING ART, AND VIBRANT CULTURE. FROM ITS UNESCO WORLD HERITAGE SITES TO ITS LIVELY FESTIVALS AND EVENTS, RAVENNA OFFERS A UNIQUE AND MEMORABLE TRAVEL EXPERIENCE.....   65
- RECOMMENDATION: IF YOU'RE PLANNING A TRIP TO RAVENNA, WE RECOMMEND TAKING THE TIME TO EXPLORE THE CITY'S UNESCO WORLD HERITAGE SITES, INCLUDING THE BASILICA DI SAN VITALE, THE MAUSOLEUM OF GALLA PLACIDIA, AND THE ARIAN BAPTISTERY. THESE ARCHITECTURAL MARVELS SHOWCASE THE CITY'S UNIQUE MOSAIC ARTISTRY AND PROVIDE A GLIMPSE INTO ITS HISTORICAL SIGNIFICANCE.....   65

General Introduction

Welcome to the captivating city of Ravenna, a hidden gem nestled in the Emilia-Romagna region of Italy. Ravenna, with its rich history, awe-inspiring art, and cultural treasures, offers a truly immersive and enchanting travel experience.

As you walk through the streets of Ravenna, you'll be transported back in time, surrounded by a fusion of Byzantine, Roman, and medieval influences. This city, once the capital of the Western Roman Empire and later the capital of Byzantine Italy, holds within its boundaries a remarkable collection of UNESCO World Heritage Sites, including some of the most dazzling mosaics in the world.

In this comprehensive travel guide, we will take you on a journey through the captivating wonders of Ravenna. We will delve into its historical significance, explore its renowned architectural masterpieces, provide practical information to enhance your visit, and offer tips on experiencing the city's vibrant culture and local traditions.

Whether you are an art enthusiast, a history lover, a culinary explorer, or simply a traveler seeking beauty and inspiration, Ravenna promises to captivate your senses and leave an indelible mark on your heart.

So, join us as we embark on a virtual tour through the cobblestone streets and intricate mosaic-adorned buildings of Ravenna. Prepare to be amazed by the artistic brilliance, delve into the stories of emperors and kings, and immerse yourself in a city that is truly a treasure trove of culture and history. Let Ravenna's ancient wonders and modern charms unfold before your eyes, as we guide you through the marvels and secrets of this remarkable city.

Chapter 1: Introduction to Ravenna

- History: Explore the rich historical background of Ravenna, known for its significant role in the Byzantine Empire.
- Location and Accessibility: Learn about Ravenna's geographical location and the various ways to reach this enchanting city.
- Climate and Best Time to Visit: Discover the ideal seasons to experience Ravenna's pleasant weather and avoid crowds

Ravenna, a small city in the Emilia-Romagna region of Italy, holds a captivating allure that stems from its historical significance and remarkable Byzantine heritage. Nestled on the eastern coast of the country, Ravenna served as the capital of the Western Roman Empire from 402 to 476 AD and later became the seat of Byzantine power in Italy. This rich historical tapestry has left an indelible mark on the city, evident in its architectural wonders and exquisite mosaics.

History: To truly appreciate Ravenna, it is essential to delve into its fascinating history. The city's importance dates back to ancient times when it was a strategic Roman port. Ravenna rose to prominence under the Roman Emperor Honorius, who moved the capital from Milan to Ravenna in 402 AD. This relocation was driven by the city's advantageous position, protected by marshlands that provided a natural defense against invading forces.

During the Byzantine period, Ravenna flourished as the capital of the Exarchate of Ravenna, which governed much of Italy from the 6th to the 8th century AD. The Byzantine emperors adorned Ravenna with magnificent structures, leaving behind an extraordinary collection of religious and secular architecture.

Location and Accessibility: Situated in northeastern Italy, Ravenna enjoys a prime location near the Adriatic Sea. The city is approximately 150 kilometers southeast of Venice and 85 kilometers east of Bologna, making it easily accessible by various means of transportation.

Travelers can reach Ravenna by air through the Bologna Guglielmo Marconi Airport, which serves domestic and international flights. From the airport, there are convenient train connections to Ravenna, with a travel time of around one hour.

Alternatively, those traveling by train can reach Ravenna directly from major Italian cities such as Milan, Florence, and Rome. The train station is located close to the city center, making it convenient for visitors to explore Ravenna upon arrival.

Climate and Best Time to Visit: Ravenna experiences a Mediterranean climate, characterized by hot summers and mild winters. The city's proximity to the sea moderates the temperatures, creating a pleasant atmosphere for most of the year.

The best time to visit Ravenna is during the spring (April to June) and autumn (September to October) seasons when the weather is mild, and the city is less crowded. These periods offer comfortable temperatures for sightseeing and allow visitors to fully appreciate the outdoor attractions and cultural events without excessive heat or cold.

Summers in Ravenna can be hot, with temperatures often exceeding 30°C (86°F). While it may be the peak tourist season, it is advisable to carry sun protection and plan visits to attractions during the cooler parts of the day.

With its captivating history, stunning mosaics, and unique cultural heritage, Ravenna awaits exploration. In the following chapters, we will embark on a journey through the city's top attractions, hidden gems, culinary delights, and practical information to make your visit to Ravenna an unforgettable experience.

Chapter 2: Top Attractions in Ravenna

- Basilica di San Vitale: Delve into the architectural masterpiece adorned with stunning mosaics that depict biblical scenes.
- Mausoleum of Galla Placidia: Experience the exquisite beauty of this mausoleum, renowned for its shimmering mosaics.
- Dante's Tomb: Pay homage to the final resting place of the famous poet Dante Alighieri, who found refuge in Ravenna.
- Basilica di Sant'Apollinare in Classe: Explore this UNESCO World Heritage Site and marvel at its intricate mosaics and ancient history.
- Neoniano Baptistery: Discover the oldest monument in Ravenna, featuring intricate baptismal scenes portrayed through mosaics.

Ravenna is a treasure trove of architectural wonders and mesmerizing mosaics that have earned it a well-deserved spot on the UNESCO World Heritage List. In this chapter, we will delve into the city's top attractions, each offering a glimpse into Ravenna's rich historical and artistic heritage.

Basilica di San Vitale: A visit to Ravenna would be incomplete without experiencing the breathtaking Basilica di San Vitale. This 6th-century Byzantine masterpiece is renowned for its intricate mosaics that depict scenes from the Bible and portray emperors and empresses. Step inside the octagonal structure and marvel at the harmonious fusion of Eastern and Western architectural elements.

Mausoleum of Galla Placidia: Prepare to be awestruck by the intimate and ethereal beauty of the Mausoleum of Galla Placidia. Built in the 5th century, this small mausoleum is adorned with shimmering mosaics featuring intricate geometric patterns and captivating depictions of biblical figures. The soft hues and intricate details make it a truly enchanting space.

Dante's Tomb: Ravenna holds a special place in literary history as the final resting place of the renowned Italian poet Dante Alighieri. Pay homage to his legacy by visiting Dante's Tomb, located within the Basilica di San

Francesco. The tomb is a symbolic tribute to one of Italy's most influential literary figures, known for his masterpiece, "The Divine Comedy."

Basilica di Sant'Apollinare in Classe: A short distance from the city center lies the Basilica di Sant'Apollinare in Classe, another UNESCO World Heritage Site. This magnificent basilica, dating back to the 6th century, showcases stunning mosaics that narrate stories from the lives of saints and martyrs.

Neoniano Baptistery: Step into the oldest monument in Ravenna, the Neoniano Baptistery, and be transported back to the early Christian era. Marvel at the well-preserved mosaics adorning the dome and witness the symbolism of baptism through intricate imagery. The baptistery's small size and intimate atmosphere make it a hidden gem worth exploring.

As you explore these top attractions, take your time to admire the craftsmanship and attention to detail found in Ravenna's mosaics. Their vibrant colors and intricate designs are testaments to the city's historical importance as a hub of Byzantine art and culture.

Ravenna's mosaic masterpieces extend beyond these highlighted sites, and you'll discover more as you wander through the city's streets and visit other churches, baptisteries, and museums. Each mosaic tells a story, transporting you back in time to the height of Ravenna's cultural and artistic splendor.

In the next chapter, we will venture into Ravenna's cultural and historical sites, where you'll encounter museums, chapels, and remnants of ancient civilizations that further enrich the city's unique heritage.

Chapter 3: Cultural and Historical Sites

- Museo Nazionale di Ravenna: Immerse yourself in Ravenna's cultural heritage through a visit to this museum, which houses an impressive collection of artifacts.
- Arian Baptistry: Uncover the remnants of the Arian Christian movement and its influence on Ravenna's history.
- Archiepiscopal Museum and Chapel: Delight in the artistic treasures preserved within this museum, including illuminated manuscripts and religious relics.
- Rocca Brancaleone: Learn about the military history of Ravenna while exploring this medieval fortress.

In addition to its renowned mosaics, Ravenna is home to a wealth of cultural and historical sites that provide deeper insights into the city's captivating past. From museums and chapels to archaeological remains, this chapter will guide you through Ravenna's remarkable treasures.

Museo Nazionale di Ravenna: Begin your cultural exploration at the Museo Nazionale di Ravenna, located in the former Benedictine monastery of Saint Vitale. This museum houses a remarkable collection of artifacts, including sculptures, early Christian sarcophagi, and exquisite Byzantine ivory carvings. Immerse yourself in the history of Ravenna as you explore the museum's carefully curated exhibits.

Arian Baptistry: Delve into Ravenna's religious history with a visit to the Arian Baptistry. Built during the Ostrogothic rule in the 5th century, this baptistry provides a fascinating glimpse into the Arian Christian movement. Admire the beautiful mosaics that adorn the interior, showcasing biblical scenes and symbolic motifs.

Archiepiscopal Museum and Chapel: Step into the Archiepiscopal Museum and Chapel, located within the Archbishop's Palace complex, and discover a treasure trove of religious art. The museum houses a remarkable collection of illuminated manuscripts, liturgical objects, and religious relics, including fragments of Ravenna's early Christian period.

Rocca Brancaleone: Uncover Ravenna's military history at the Rocca Brancaleone, a medieval fortress built in the 15th century. Originally constructed for defensive purposes, this imposing structure now hosts exhibitions and cultural events. Explore the fortress's battlements, towers, and inner courtyard, and gain a glimpse into Ravenna's medieval past.

Domus dei Tappeti di Pietra: Discover a hidden gem in the heart of Ravenna as you visit the Domus dei Tappeti di Pietra (House of Stone Carpets). Excavated beneath the city streets, this archaeological site offers a fascinating glimpse into Roman life. Walk along the ancient paths, marvel at the preserved mosaics, and imagine the bustling city that once stood above.

Basilica di San Francesco: A visit to Ravenna would not be complete without exploring the Basilica di San Francesco. This church, dating back to the 10th century, showcases a harmonious blend of Romanesque and Gothic architectural styles. Inside, you'll find stunning frescoes depicting scenes from the life of Saint Francis of Assisi, as well as beautiful Byzantine-influenced mosaics.

As you explore these cultural and historical sites, take the time to absorb the atmosphere, appreciate the artistry, and uncover the stories woven into the fabric of Ravenna's past. Each site offers a unique perspective on the city's vibrant history and its significance in shaping the cultural landscape of Italy.

Sant'Apollinare Nuovo: Visit the Basilica of Sant'Apollinare Nuovo, an early Christian church renowned for its extensive mosaics. Admire the vibrant scenes depicting biblical narratives and the procession of saints that adorn the nave, providing a captivating visual representation of Ravenna's artistic heritage.

Theodoric's Mausoleum: Explore the Mausoleum of Theodoric, an impressive burial monument built in the 6th century for the Ostrogothic king Theodoric the Great. This circular structure with its unique blend of

Roman and Gothic architecture stands as a testament to the Gothic Kingdom's influence in Ravenna.

Domus dei Tappeti di Pietra - Domus dei Tritons: Continue your journey beneath the streets of Ravenna with a visit to the Domus dei Tritons (House of the Tritons). This archaeological site reveals the remains of a luxurious Roman villa, featuring intricate mosaic floors depicting marine motifs, including tritons and sea creatures.

Dante Alighieri's Quadrarco: Explore the Quadrarco di Braccioforte, an ancient Roman arch that serves as a tribute to the renowned poet Dante Alighieri. This structure is said to mark the location of Dante's house during his exile in Ravenna, honoring his connection to the city.

Teodorico Ravenna's Archaeological Park: Embark on a journey through Ravenna's past by visiting the Teodorico Ravenna Archaeological Park. This expansive outdoor park encompasses the remnants of ancient Roman structures, including a Roman road, a mausoleum, and the remains of a Roman port.

Rasponi Crypt: Delve into Ravenna's subterranean secrets with a visit to the Rasponi Crypt. Located beneath the Church of San Francesco, this hidden crypt houses numerous sarcophagi and serves as the final resting place for noble families of Ravenna.

These additional sites offer a deeper understanding of Ravenna's cultural and historical significance, providing a glimpse into different periods of the city's past. As you explore these remarkable sites, you'll gain a greater appreciation for Ravenna's rich heritage and its enduring legacy as a hub of art, culture, and history.

In the upcoming chapter, we will venture into the distinct neighborhoods of Ravenna, each offering its own unique charm and allure. From the bustling city center to the tranquil countryside, you'll discover the diverse facets of this captivating city.

Chapter 4: Exploring Ravenna's Neighborhoods

- Ravenna City Center: Stroll through the lively streets and picturesque squares of the city center, experiencing the local atmosphere and vibrant markets.
- Classis Ravenna: Discover the ancient Roman port of Ravenna, with its archaeological remains and captivating historical sites.
- Marina di Ravenna: Escape to the coast and enjoy the beautiful beaches, waterfront promenades, and fresh seafood cuisine.
- Sant'Apollinare: Visit the charming village surrounding the basilica, and admire the rural landscapes of the Ravenna countryside.

Ravenna is a city of diverse neighborhoods, each with its own distinctive character and attractions. From the vibrant city center to the charming countryside, this chapter will guide you through the different neighborhoods of Ravenna, offering a glimpse into their unique charm and allure.

Ravenna City Center: Begin your exploration in the heart of Ravenna, the city center. This bustling area is a treasure trove of historical sites, lively squares, and vibrant streets. Take a leisurely stroll along Via Cavour, the main thoroughfare, lined with shops, cafes, and boutiques. Explore Piazza del Popolo, the central square, and marvel at the stunning architecture of the Palazzo del Municipio (Town Hall). Don't forget to visit the bustling Mercato Coperto, an indoor market where you can sample local products and soak up the lively atmosphere.

Classis Ravenna: Venture beyond the city center to Classis Ravenna, the ancient Roman port of Ravenna. This neighborhood is a treasure trove of archaeological remains and historical sites. Explore the remains of the Roman city walls and gateways, such as Porta Serrata and Porta San Mama. Visit the archaeological park, which showcases the ruins of warehouses, docks, and other structures from Ravenna's maritime past. Classis Ravenna offers a fascinating glimpse into the city's ancient history and its significance as a bustling port.

Marina di Ravenna: For a change of scenery, head to Marina di Ravenna, located on the coast. This neighborhood is a popular destination for beach lovers and water enthusiasts. Enjoy long stretches of sandy beaches, where you can relax, swim, or soak up the sun. Take a leisurely stroll along the promenade, lined with shops, bars, and restaurants. Indulge in delicious seafood cuisine, and savor the fresh catch of the day. Marina di Ravenna offers a perfect blend of seaside charm and coastal relaxation.

Sant'Apollinare: Just a short distance from the city center lies the charming village of Sant'Apollinare. This neighborhood is centered around the stunning Basilica di Sant'Apollinare in Classe, a UNESCO World Heritage Site. Explore the peaceful streets, admire the traditional architecture, and enjoy the tranquil ambiance. Sant'Apollinare offers a serene retreat from the bustle of the city, and its proximity to the countryside provides an opportunity to immerse yourself in Ravenna's rural landscapes.

Each neighborhood of Ravenna offers a unique experience, showcasing different aspects of the city's cultural and natural beauty. Whether you're exploring the historical sites in the city center, discovering the ancient Roman port in Classis Ravenna, enjoying the coastal charm of Marina di Ravenna, or finding tranquility in Sant'Apollinare, each neighborhood has something special to offer.

San Vitale: Located near the city center, the San Vitale neighborhood is named after the famous Basilica di San Vitale. This area exudes a peaceful atmosphere with its tree-lined streets and charming residential buildings. Take a leisurely stroll through the neighborhood and admire the beautiful architecture. San Vitale is also home to several local shops, cafes, and trattorias where you can savor traditional Ravennate cuisine.

Borgo San Rocco: Step into the artistic neighborhood of Borgo San Rocco, known for its vibrant street art and creative atmosphere. This bohemian district is adorned with colorful murals and graffiti, transforming the streets into an open-air art gallery. Explore the narrow alleys and discover unique art studios, galleries, and artisan workshops. Borgo San Rocco is a haven for art enthusiasts and offers a dynamic and inspiring environment.

Borgo Marina: Nestled along the canal, Borgo Marina is a picturesque neighborhood that combines history and natural beauty. Take a leisurely stroll along the waterfront promenade and admire the colorful boats and charming houses. Discover small seafood restaurants and cafes where you can indulge in local delicacies, such as freshly caught fish and seafood pasta. Enjoy the tranquil ambiance and soak up the scenic views of the canal.

Roncalceci: For those seeking a peaceful retreat amidst nature, the Roncalceci neighborhood is the perfect destination. Located in the countryside surrounding Ravenna, this area offers vast open spaces, rolling hills, and vineyards. Take a scenic drive or bike ride through the countryside and discover the beauty of the rural landscapes. Roncalceci is also known for its vineyards, producing excellent wines such as Sangiovese and Albana. Visit local wineries for wine tastings and experience the rich flavors of Ravenna's renowned wines.

Pilastro: Experience a traditional village atmosphere in the Pilastro neighborhood, located on the outskirts of Ravenna. This rustic area is known for its agricultural heritage and charming farmhouses. Explore the village and witness local artisans at work, producing traditional products such as handmade ceramics and artisanal food items. Pilastro offers a glimpse into the rural traditions and agricultural practices that are an integral part of Ravenna's identity.

Exploring the various neighborhoods of Ravenna allows you to experience the city from different perspectives, whether it's immersing yourself in its historical center, enjoying the coastal charm, discovering artistic enclaves, or savoring the tranquility of the countryside. Each neighborhood adds a unique flavor to your Ravenna adventure, making your visit even more enriching and memorable.

In the next chapter, we will tantalize your taste buds with a culinary journey through Ravenna, showcasing the local dishes, specialty ingredients, and traditional recipes that define the gastronomic landscape of the city.

Chapter 5: Gastronomic Delights of Ravenna

- Local Cuisine: Indulge in Ravenna's traditional dishes, including homemade pasta, piadina (flatbread), and delicious seafood recipes.
- Wines and Wineries: Embark on a journey through the local vineyards and taste the unique wines produced in the region.
- Pasticcerie: Sample Ravenna's renowned pastries, such as the aromatic ciambella and the sweet delicacy called piada dolce.

Ravenna's culinary scene is a delightful fusion of traditional Italian flavors and regional specialties. In this chapter, we will embark on a mouthwatering journey through the gastronomic treasures of the city, exploring the local dishes, specialty ingredients, and traditional recipes that make Ravenna a true food lover's paradise.

Piadina Romagnola: One cannot talk about Ravenna's cuisine without mentioning the iconic Piadina Romagnola. This thin, unleavened flatbread is a staple in the region and is typically filled with a variety of savory ingredients such as cured meats, cheese, and vegetables. Indulge in the simple yet satisfying flavors of a freshly made piadina, a true symbol of Romagna's culinary heritage.

Cappelletti: Cappelletti, also known as "little hats," are a traditional pasta dish hailing from Ravenna. These small, hat-shaped pasta pockets are typically filled with a mixture of meat, cheese, and herbs. Served in a rich broth or topped with a savory sauce, cappelletti are a comforting and flavorful delight that embodies the essence of traditional Ravennate cuisine.

Passatelli: Another beloved pasta dish in Ravenna is Passatelli, a specialty that combines breadcrumbs, eggs, cheese, and nutmeg to form a unique pasta dough. Passatelli are typically cooked in a rich broth and often accompanied by grated Parmigiano-Reggiano cheese. The result is a hearty and comforting dish, perfect for warming the soul on a chilly day.

Piadina Farcita: Building upon the foundation of the beloved Piadina Romagnola, the Piadina Farcita takes this traditional flatbread to another level. It is filled with a variety of mouthwatering ingredients, such as cured meats, local cheeses, fresh vegetables, and delectable spreads like squacquerone cheese or olive paste. The Piadina Farcita is a customizable delight that satisfies both hunger and culinary curiosity.

Brodetto di Pesce: As a coastal city, Ravenna boasts an abundance of fresh seafood, and Brodetto di Pesce is a dish that showcases the flavors of the Adriatic Sea. This traditional fish stew is made with a variety of local fish, such as scorpionfish, monkfish, and cuttlefish, cooked in a fragrant tomato-based broth. Served with a slice of toasted bread, Brodetto di Pesce is a true taste of the sea.

Squacquerone: Squacquerone is a soft and creamy cheese that holds a special place in Ravenna's culinary heritage. Made from cow's milk, this delicate cheese has a mild and slightly tangy flavor. It is often spread on Piadina or enjoyed as a topping for bread and vegetables. Don't miss the opportunity to savor the local Squacquerone, as it adds a delightful creaminess to many dishes.

Sangiovese Wine: No gastronomic journey through Ravenna is complete without indulging in the region's renowned wines. Ravenna is located in the Emilia-Romagna region, known for its exceptional wine production. Sample the local Sangiovese wine, a red wine with a robust character, often featuring notes of cherry and spice. Pair it with the rich flavors of Ravenna's cuisine for a truly exquisite dining experience.

Throughout Ravenna, you'll find numerous trattorias, osterias, and local markets where you can savor these traditional dishes and discover even more culinary delights. The city's gastronomic scene is a celebration of simple yet flavorful ingredients, prepared with love and respect for

Rustida di Pesce: Rustida di Pesce is a delightful seafood dish that is popular in Ravenna. It consists of marinated and grilled fish, typically sea bass or gilt-head bream, seasoned with aromatic herbs and lemon. The fish is cooked to perfection, resulting in a succulent and flavorful dish that highlights the natural flavors of the sea.

Torta al Testo: Torta al Testo is a traditional bread-like flatcake that is a beloved specialty of the region. It is made from a simple dough of flour, water, and salt, cooked on a round, cast-iron griddle called a testo. The torta is often split and filled with various savory ingredients like prosciutto, cheese, and greens, creating a satisfying and delicious sandwich.

Albana Passito Wine: For wine enthusiasts with a sweet tooth, Albana Passito is a dessert wine that should not be missed. Made from late-harvested Albana grapes, this golden nectar is rich and aromatic, with notes of honey, apricot, and dried fruits. Pair it with a selection of local cheeses or desserts for a decadent and indulgent experience.

Ciambella: Ciambella is a traditional ring-shaped cake that is a staple of Ravenna's dessert offerings. This simple yet delightful treat is made with flour, sugar, eggs, and lemon zest, resulting in a moist and tender cake with a hint of citrus flavor. Enjoy a slice of ciambella with a cup of coffee or as a sweet ending to a meal.

Friggione: Friggione is a savory vegetable stew that showcases the flavors of Ravenna's countryside. It is made with slow-cooked onions, tomatoes, and bell peppers, seasoned with herbs and spices. Friggione is a versatile dish that can be enjoyed as a side dish or served as a sauce over pasta or polenta, offering a taste of the region's agricultural bounty.

Ravenna's culinary landscape is a true reflection of the region's rich history, traditional recipes, and locally sourced ingredients. From the simplicity of Piadina Romagnola to the complexity of Brodetto di Pesce, each dish tells a story and invites you to savor the unique flavors of Ravenna. So indulge in the gastronomic delights, discover new taste sensations, and let the culinary traditions of Ravenna enchant your palate.

In the next chapter, we will delve into the vibrant events and festivals that take place in Ravenna throughout the year. From historical reenactments to lively cultural celebrations, you'll have the opportunity to immerse yourself in the city's dynamic and festive spirit.

Chapter 6: Festivals and Events in Ravenna

- Ravenna Festival: The Ravenna Festival is a renowned international event that celebrates the arts in all its forms.
- Mosaico di Notte: Mosaico di Notte, or Mosaic by Night, is a unique event that takes place in Ravenna during the summer months
- Festa di San Vitale: The Festa di San Vitale, celebrated on April 28th, is a religious festival dedicated to Ravenna's patron saint, Saint Vitalis.
- Rombi di Passione: Rombi di Passione, or Rhombuses of Passion, is a medieval festival that takes place in the village of Sant'Apollinare, just outside Ravenna.
- Ravenna Nightmare Film Festival: For horror movie enthusiasts, the Ravenna Nightmare Film Festival is a must-attend event.

Ravenna is a city that comes alive with vibrant festivals and events throughout the year. From historical reenactments to cultural celebrations, this chapter will guide you through some of the most exciting and memorable festivities that take place in Ravenna, offering you a chance to immerse yourself in the city's dynamic and festive spirit.

Ravenna Festival: The Ravenna Festival is a renowned international event that celebrates the arts in all its forms. Held annually from late spring to early summer, the festival features a diverse program of concerts, opera performances, dance shows, theater productions, and art exhibitions. Artists and performers from around the world gather in Ravenna to showcase their talents, creating a captivating atmosphere of creativity and cultural exchange.

Mosaico di Notte: Mosaico di Notte, or Mosaic by Night, is a unique event that takes place in Ravenna during the summer months. The city's extraordinary mosaic masterpieces are illuminated, allowing visitors to experience the beauty of these ancient artworks in a different light. Guided tours and special exhibitions are organized to provide deeper insights into the history and techniques of mosaic art. Stroll through the illuminated streets and squares, marvel at the intricate mosaic designs, and witness the city's rich artistic heritage come to life after dark.

Festa di San Vitale: The Festa di San Vitale, celebrated on April 28th, is a religious festival dedicated to Ravenna's patron saint, Saint Vitalis. The festivities include a solemn procession through the city streets, led by the archbishop and accompanied by religious icons and the faithful. The celebration is an opportunity for locals and visitors alike to witness the deep religious devotion and experience the rich cultural traditions of Ravenna.

Rombi di Passione: Rombi di Passione, or Rhombuses of Passion, is a medieval festival that takes place in the village of Sant'Apollinare, just outside Ravenna. Held in May, this lively event reenacts medieval life and customs through music, dance, theater performances, and historical demonstrations. Colorful costumes, traditional games, and delicious food create a festive atmosphere, immersing visitors in the spirit of the Middle Ages.

Sagra del Pesce: The Sagra del Pesce, or Fish Festival, is a culinary celebration that pays homage to Ravenna's coastal heritage and abundant seafood. This annual event, held in Marina di Ravenna in July, offers a wide array of seafood dishes prepared by local chefs and fishermen. Enjoy fresh catches of the day, from fried fish to seafood risotto, while soaking up the lively atmosphere of the festival and taking in the stunning views of the Adriatic Sea.

Ravenna Nightmare Film Festival: For horror movie enthusiasts, the Ravenna Nightmare Film Festival is a must-attend event. Held in October, this international film festival showcases a selection of horror, fantasy, and science fiction films from around the world. From classic cult favorites to innovative indie productions, the festival provides a thrilling cinematic experience for fans of the genre.

Christmas Markets: During the holiday season, Ravenna comes alive with charming Christmas markets that add a touch of festive magic to the city. The markets feature stalls selling traditional crafts, local products, and delicious treats. Explore the festive decorations, listen to Christmas carols, and find unique gifts and souvenirs to bring home.

These are just a few of the many festivals and events that take place in Ravenna throughout the year. Each celebration offers a unique glimpse into the city's cultural, artistic, and culinary heritage, allowing you to experience Ravenna's vibrant spirit and immerse yourself in its rich traditions.

Chapter 7: Practical Information and Travel Tips

- Bologna: Venture beyond Ravenna and explore the vibrant city of Bologna, famous for its rich history, cuisine, and medieval architecture.
- Ferrara: Visit this charming Renaissance city, known for its well-preserved historic center and imposing Este Castle.

When visiting Ravenna, it's essential to have some practical information and travel tips to make your trip smooth and enjoyable. In this chapter, we will provide you with valuable information on transportation, accommodations, local festivals and events, as well as shopping and souvenirs, ensuring that you have a memorable experience in the city.

Transportation: Ravenna is a relatively compact city, and most of its attractions are within walking distance from each other. However, if you prefer public transportation, the city has a reliable bus network that covers the main areas of interest. You can purchase tickets at tobacco shops, newsstands, or directly from the bus driver. Alternatively, renting a bicycle is a popular and eco-friendly way to explore Ravenna. The city has well-marked cycling routes and offers bike rental services.

Accommodations: Ravenna offers a range of accommodations to suit various budgets and preferences. In the city center, you'll find charming boutique hotels, guesthouses, and bed and breakfasts. If you're looking for a more luxurious experience, there are upscale hotels that provide excellent amenities and services. For budget-conscious travelers, there are affordable options such as hostels and budget hotels. Local Festivals and Events: To fully immerse yourself in the local culture, try to coincide your visit with one of Ravenna's vibrant festivals or events. As mentioned in Chapter 6, the Ravenna Festival in late spring and Mosaico di Notte during the summer months are major highlights. Keep an eye out for other events such as historical reenactments, music concerts, and food festivals that take place throughout the year. Check the local tourism website or inquire at your accommodation for the latest information on upcoming events.

Shopping and Souvenirs: Ravenna offers fantastic shopping opportunities, whether you're looking for souvenirs or unique local products. The city is known for its traditional handicrafts, including mosaic art, ceramics, and handwoven textiles. Explore the artisan shops and boutiques in the city center to find authentic and high-quality items. The local markets, such as Mercato Coperto and Piazza Andrea Costa Market, are also worth a visit for fresh produce, local delicacies, and regional specialties.

Safety and Etiquette: Ravenna is generally a safe city for travelers, but it's always advisable to take standard safety precautions. It's also important to respect local customs and etiquette. Dress modestly when visiting religious sites, and be mindful of noise levels, particularly during siesta hours when some businesses may be closed for a break.

Local Customs and Language: Italian is the official language in Ravenna, and while English is spoken in most tourist areas, learning a few basic Italian phrases can enhance your interactions with locals. Italians value politeness and greeting with a "buongiorno" (good morning) or "buonasera" (good evening) is always appreciated. It's customary to say "grazie" (thank you) and "prego" (you're welcome) when interacting with service staff.

By familiarizing yourself with these practical tips, you'll be well-prepared to navigate Ravenna and make the most of your visit. Whether you're exploring the city's attractions, attending local festivals, or shopping for souvenirs, these insights will help ensure a memorable and enjoyable experience.

Dining and Cuisine: Ravenna is a culinary paradise, and exploring the local cuisine is a must. Look for trattorias and osterias that offer traditional Ravennate dishes, such as piadina, cappelletti, and brodetto di pesce. Don't forget to pair your meal with a glass of local Sangiovese wine or try the Albana Passito for a sweet treat. It's customary to leave a small tip, around 10% of the total bill, as a token of appreciation for good service.

Opening Hours and Holidays: Most shops, attractions, and restaurants in Ravenna follow regular business hours, opening around 9:00 AM and closing in the evening. However, it's important to note that some establishments, particularly smaller shops and family-owned businesses, may close for a midday break. Additionally, be aware that many shops are closed on Sundays, except during the peak tourist season. On public holidays, such as Easter Monday or Christmas Day, some places may have reduced hours or be closed entirely.

Climate and What to Pack: Ravenna experiences a Mediterranean climate, characterized by hot summers and mild winters. If you're visiting during the summer months, pack lightweight and breathable clothing, sunscreen, a hat, and sunglasses. In spring and autumn, it's advisable to have layers as the weather can be unpredictable. For winter visits, bring a coat, scarf, and gloves, as temperatures can be chilly. Don't forget comfortable walking shoes for exploring the city's attractions.

Currency and Payment Methods: The official currency in Ravenna, as in the rest of Italy, is the Euro (€). Credit cards are widely accepted in hotels, restaurants, and larger shops, but it's always good to carry some cash, especially for small establishments, markets, or local vendors. ATMs can be found throughout the city, allowing you to withdraw cash as needed. Notify your bank or credit card company of your travel plans to avoid any issues with using your cards abroad.

Getting Around the Region: If you have extra time during your visit to Ravenna, consider exploring the surrounding region of Emilia-Romagna. The region is well-connected by train, allowing you to visit cities like Bologna, Ferrara, and Rimini easily. Each city has its own unique attractions, culinary specialties, and cultural experiences, providing you with a broader perspective of the area's diversity and charm.

By incorporating these additional practical tips into your Ravenna travel plans, you'll be well-prepared to navigate the city, engage with the local customs, and make the most of your experience. Enjoy your time in Ravenna, and may your journey be filled with wonderful memories and discoveries.

Chapter 8: Day Trips from Ravenna

- Bologna: Located just a short train ride away from Ravenna, Bologna is a vibrant city known for its historic architecture, culinary delights, and lively atmosphere.
- Ferrara: Another charming city within reach of Ravenna is Ferrara. Famous for its well-preserved Renaissance architecture and impressive Este Castle, Ferrara offers a glimpse into Italy's glorious past
- Rimini: For those seeking a beachside escape, Rimini is an excellent choice. Known for its long sandy beaches and vibrant nightlife
- San Marino: A short journey from Ravenna will take you to the tiny and independent Republic of San Marino, one of the world's oldest surviving sovereign states
- Brisighella: Located in the Apennine Mountains, Brisighella is a charming medieval village with a distinctive three-peaked hill.

While Ravenna offers a wealth of attractions and experiences, taking day trips to nearby destinations allows you to further explore the beauty and cultural richness of the region. In this chapter, we will highlight some captivating places that are perfect for day trips from Ravenna.

Bologna: Located just a short train ride away from Ravenna, Bologna is a vibrant city known for its historic architecture, culinary delights, and lively atmosphere. Explore the city's medieval center, Piazza Maggiore, and the iconic Two Towers. Don't miss the chance to visit the University of Bologna, one of the oldest universities in the world. Indulge in Bologna's gastronomic offerings, including tortellini, mortadella, and gelato, and immerse yourself in the city's rich cultural heritage.

Ferrara: Another charming city within reach of Ravenna is Ferrara. Famous for its well-preserved Renaissance architecture and impressive Este Castle, Ferrara offers a glimpse into Italy's glorious past. Stroll along the picturesque streets of the city center, visit the magnificent Ferrara Cathedral, and explore the fascinating Jewish Quarter. Take a bike ride along the city walls, which are among the best-preserved in Europe, and experience the unique atmosphere of this UNESCO World Heritage Site.

Rimini: For those seeking a beachside escape, Rimini is an excellent choice. Rimini offers a mix of relaxation and entertainment. Soak up the sun, swim in the Adriatic Sea, or explore the city's historical sites, such as the Arch of Augustus and the Malatesta Temple. Take a stroll along the lively promenade, visit the Grand Hotel, and indulge in delicious seafood at one of the many beachfront restaurants.

San Marino: A short journey from Ravenna will take you to the tiny and independent Republic of San Marino, one of the world's oldest surviving sovereign states. Perched atop Mount Titano, San Marino offers breathtaking panoramic views of the surrounding countryside. Explore the historic center, stroll through the charming streets, and visit the impressive medieval fortress, Guaita Tower. Enjoy duty-free shopping and pick up unique souvenirs to commemorate your visit.

Comacchio: Nestled in the Po Delta, Comacchio is a picturesque town known as "Little Venice" due to its canals and bridges. Discover the historic center with its colorful buildings, explore the Trepponti Bridge, and visit the ancient Cathedral of San Cassiano. Take a boat tour through the canals and observe the rich birdlife in the nearby wetlands. Comacchio offers a peaceful and enchanting escape from the bustling city, allowing you to connect with nature and enjoy a slower pace.

Brisighella: Located in the Apennine Mountains, Brisighella is a charming medieval village with a distinctive three-peaked hill. Explore the narrow streets, admire the well-preserved architecture, and visit the Rocca Manfrediana fortress. Don't miss the opportunity to take a walk along the "Via degli Asini," an ancient path lined with olive trees, and enjoy breathtaking views of the surrounding countryside. Brisighella is also famous for its olive oil production, so be sure to sample some of the local delicacies.

These day trips from Ravenna provide a diverse range of experiences, allowing you to discover the historical, cultural, and natural wonders of the region. Whether you're exploring the vibrant city of Bologna, relaxing on the beaches of Rimini, or immersing yourself in the medieval charm of Ferrara, each destination offers a unique perspective and enriches your journey in Emilia-Romagna.

Chapter 9: Tips for a Memorable Stay in Ravenna

- Plan Ahead
- Guided Tours
- Explore on Foot or by Bike
- Sample Local Cuisine
- Visit Lesser-Known Attractions
- Use Public Transportation or Walk...

Plan Ahead: Before your trip to Ravenna, research the city's top attractions, opening hours, and any special events taking place during your visit. Create an itinerary that allows you to make the most of your time and prioritize the sights that interest you the most.

Guided Tours: Consider joining a guided tour to gain deeper insights into Ravenna's history, art, and culture. Knowledgeable guides can provide fascinating information and stories that enhance your experience of the city's landmarks and treasures.

Explore on Foot or by Bike: Ravenna is a pedestrian-friendly city, and exploring its streets on foot allows you to discover hidden gems and appreciate the beauty of its architecture. Renting a bike is another great option, as it allows you to cover more ground and explore the city at a leisurely pace.

Sample Local Cuisine: Ravenna is known for its delectable cuisine, so be sure to indulge in local dishes and flavors. Explore the trattorias and osterias to try traditional Ravennate specialties such as piadina, cappelletti, and seafood dishes.

Visit Lesser-Known Attractions: While Ravenna's UNESCO World Heritage Sites are must-visit landmarks, consider exploring some of the lesser-known attractions as well. These include smaller churches, charming squares, and off-the-beaten-path spots that offer a more intimate and authentic experience of the city.

Ravenna on a Budget

Free Attractions: Ravenna offers several free attractions, such as the Basilica di San Vitale courtyard and the Mausoleum of Galla Placidia garden. Take advantage of these opportunities to experience the city's historical and artistic treasures without spending a dime.

Picnic in the Parks: Ravenna has beautiful parks and green spaces where you can enjoy a budget-friendly picnic. Pack a lunch with local products from markets or grocery stores and relax in the shade of the trees.

Affordable Eateries: Look for trattorias and local cafes that offer affordable menus or daily specials. These establishments often serve delicious, authentic cuisine at reasonable prices, allowing you to experience the local flavors without breaking the bank.

Recommended Souvenirs

Mosaic Art: Ravenna is famous for its stunning mosaic art, so consider bringing home a small mosaic piece or a mosaic-inspired item, such as a coaster or a decorative tile, as a unique and meaningful souvenir.

Local Food and Wine: Bring a taste of Ravenna back home by purchasing local products such as olive oil, wine, or traditional food items like piadina or homemade pasta. These make great gifts for family and friends or a reminder of your culinary experiences in Ravenna.

Local Events and Festivals

Stay updated on the local events and festivals happening during your visit to Ravenna. Check the official tourism website or local event listings for information on concerts, art exhibitions, and cultural festivals. Attending these events allows you to immerse yourself in the city's vibrant atmosphere and connect with its artistic and cultural heritage.

Sustainable Travel in Ravenna

Use Public Transportation or Walk: Opt for public transportation, cycling, or walking whenever possible to reduce your carbon footprint and explore Ravenna in an eco-friendly way. The city's compact size makes it ideal for walking, and there are well-maintained cycling routes available.

Support Local and Sustainable Businesses: Choose accommodations, restaurants, and shops that prioritize sustainability and support the local economy. Look for establishments that emphasize locally sourced ingredients,

Chapter 10. Conclusion and recommendation

- Conclusion: Ravenna is a city that captivates visitors with its rich history, breathtaking art, and vibrant culture. From its UNESCO World Heritage Sites to its lively festivals and events, Ravenna offers a unique and memorable travel experience…..
- Recommendation: If you're planning a trip to Ravenna, we recommend taking the time to explore the city's UNESCO World Heritage Sites, including the Basilica di San Vitale, the Mausoleum of Galla Placidia, and the Arian Baptistery. These architectural marvels showcase the city's unique mosaic artistry and provide a glimpse into its historical significance…..

Conclusion:

Ravenna is a city that captivates visitors with its rich history, breathtaking art, and vibrant culture. From its UNESCO World Heritage Sites to its lively festivals and events, Ravenna offers a unique and memorable travel experience. Through this travel guide, we have explored the city's top attractions, provided insights into its art and history, offered practical information and travel tips, and highlighted exciting day trips.

With its magnificent mosaics, awe-inspiring monuments, and enchanting atmosphere, Ravenna truly deserves a place on every traveler's bucket list. Whether you're an art enthusiast, a history buff, a food lover, or simply seeking a place of beauty and inspiration, Ravenna has something to offer.

Recommendation:

If you're planning a trip to Ravenna, we recommend taking the time to explore the city's UNESCO World Heritage Sites, including the Basilica di San Vitale, the Mausoleum of Galla Placidia, and the Arian Baptistery. These architectural marvels showcase the city's unique mosaic artistry and provide a glimpse into its historical significance.

Additionally, make sure to visit the Ravenna National Museum, where you can delve deeper into the city's history and admire an impressive collection of artifacts.

Don't miss the opportunity to attend the Ravenna Festival or the Mosaico di Notte events, which offer a chance to experience the city's cultural vibrancy.

As you wander through Ravenna's streets, take the time to savor the local cuisine, indulge in traditional dishes, and sample the region's wines. Immerse yourself in the city's ambiance by exploring its charming neighborhoods, browsing the local markets, and interacting with the friendly locals.

Lastly, consider taking day trips to nearby destinations such as Bologna, Ferrara, or Rimini to expand your experience of Emilia-Romagna's rich cultural heritage.

In conclusion, Ravenna is a treasure trove of art, history, and culture that promises an unforgettable journey. Let the city's mosaics, monuments, and festivals leave a lasting impression as you explore its enchanting streets and immerse yourself in its captivating atmosphere

Made in the USA
Las Vegas, NV
05 February 2025